Living in the
African Savannah

Nicola Barber

www.raintreepublishers.co.uk
Visit our website to find out more information about **Raintree** books.

To order:
☎ Phone 44 (0) 1865 888112
▤ Send a fax to 44 (0) 1865 314091
▭ Visit the Raintree bookshop at **www.raintreepublishers.co.uk** to browse our catalogue and order online.

First published in Great Britain by Raintree, Halley Court, Jordan Hill, Oxford OX2 8EJ, part of Pearson Education. Raintree is a registered trademark of Pearson Education Ltd.

© Pearson Education Ltd 2008
First published in paperback in 2009
The moral right of the proprietor has been asserted.

Editorial: Catherine Veitch
Design: Richard Parker and Manhattan Design
Illustration: International Mapping
Picture Research: Hannah Taylor and Maria Joannou
Production: Alison Parsons

Originated by Modern Age
Printed and bound in China by CTPS

ISBN 978-1 4062 0822 1 (hardback)
12 11 10 09 08
10 9 8 7 6 5 4 3 2 1

ISBN 978-1 4062 0832 0 (paperback)
12 11 10 09 08
10 9 8 7 6 5 4 3 2 1

British Library Cataloguing in Publication Data
Barber, Nicola
Living in the African savannah. - (World cultures)
967'.009153

A full catalogue record for this book is available from the British Library.

Acknowledgements
The publishers would like to thank the following for permission to reproduce photographs: Alamy Images pp. **26** (Gary Cook), **27** (Jam World Images); Corbis pp. **4** (DLILLC), **13** (Yann Arthus-Bertrand), **18** (Diego Lezama Orezzoli), **19** (Yann Arthus-Bertrand); Digital Vision p. **7**; Exile Images/ H. Davies p. **22**; Eye Ubiquitous/ Hutchison p. **11**; FLPA/ Ariadne Van Zandbergen pp. **12, 15**; Getty Images pp. **14** (Gallo Images), **24** (The Image Bank); Harcourt Education Ltd/ Tudor Photography pp. **20, 21** (left and right), **23** (all); Nature Picture Library/ Bruce Davidson p. **25**; Panos Pictures/ Karen Robinson p. **9**; Reuters pp. **8** (Antony Njuguna), **17** (Radu Sigheti); Tips Images/ Carlo Mari p. **10**; Topham Picturepoint/ The Image Works/ Louise Gubb p. **16**.

Cover photograph of a Masaai herdsman in a national park in Kenya, reproduced with permission of Corbis/ Dave Bartruff.

Maasai bracelet pp. 20-21 devised and made by Natalie Abadzis.

The publishers would like to thank Karen Morrison for her assistance with the preparation of this book.

Every effort has been made to contact copyright holders of any material reproduced in this book. Any omissions will be rectified in subsequent printings if notice is given to the publishers.

Contents

Some words are printed in bold, **like this**. You can find out what they mean on page 31.

Who are the Maasai?

The Maasai people live in East Africa. They first came from the valley of the River Nile, from the area that is now Sudan. Today, most of the Maasai live in Kenya. Some also live in northern Tanzania (see map on page 5). They are divided into different tribes called **clans**. They share a language called *Olmaa*.

▲ A group of Maasai women celebrate the opening of a new village.

The Maasai rely on cattle to make a living, and for food. They are **semi-nomadic**, moving around for parts of the year. They move to find land where their cattle can **graze** (feed).

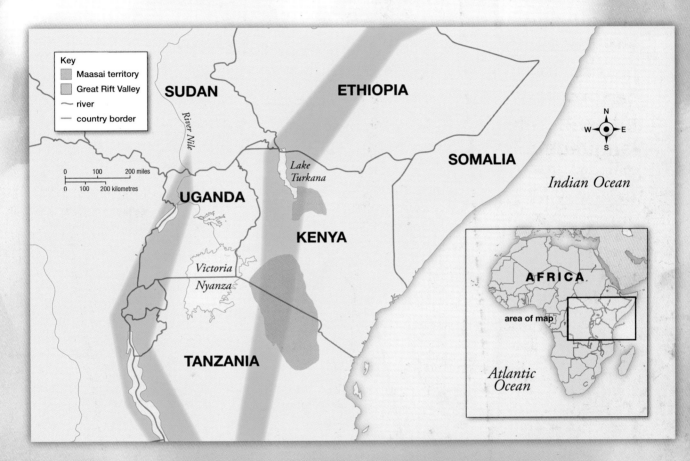

▲ The Maasai live in a small area of East Africa.

MAASAI CREATION

The Maasai tell a story about their creation. God had three sons and he gave them each a stick. The youngest was his favourite. God gave him a stick for herding cattle, and a rope. All the cattle slid down the rope from heaven to earth. This son became the first Maasai. The Maasai believe that cattle are a gift from God.

Where do the Maasai live?

The Maasai live on wide, open grasslands called the **savannah**. The savannah lie in the Great Rift Valley. The Great Rift Valley is actually a number of valleys that run from southwest Asia through eastern Africa (see map below).

The climate of the savannah is **semi-arid**. This means it is always warm or hot. There are two rainy seasons, when it rains most days. The short rainy season is in November. The longer rainy season lasts from around March to May. If the rains do not come, there is often **drought**. This means there is little or no water.

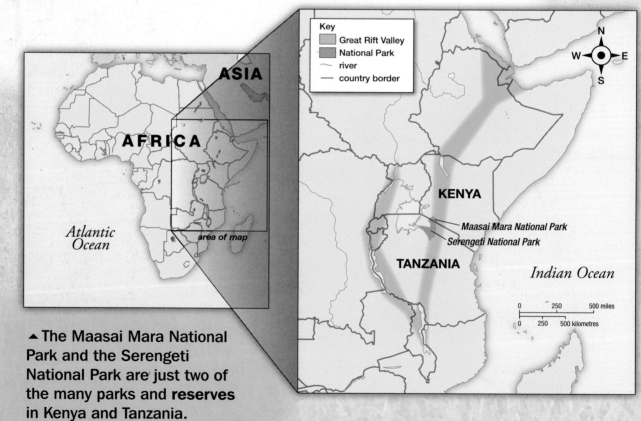

Key
  Great Rift Valley
  National Park
  river
  country border

ASIA

AFRICA

Atlantic Ocean

area of map

KENYA

Maasai Mara National Park
Serengeti National Park

TANZANIA

Indian Ocean

0   250   500 miles
0   250   500 kilometres

▲ The Maasai Mara National Park and the Serengeti National Park are just two of the many parks and **reserves** in Kenya and Tanzania.

▲ Giraffes live on the savannah of East Africa.

SAVANNAH WILDLIFE

The grassy savannah provides food for many animals. There are wildebeest, zebra, lions, giraffes, and elephants. Many animals live in protected areas called **national parks**, such as the Maasai Mara National Park in Kenya, and the Serengeti National Park in Tanzania (see map on opposite page).

Keeping cattle

The Maasai believe that cattle are a gift given to them by God. Cattle are very important to the Maasai. Cattle are often used to measure a person's wealth. A Maasai with a lot of cattle is thought to be rich.

The Maasai eat a lot of animal products such as milk and blood from their cattle. Cattle meat is only eaten on important occasions.

▲ Maasai men take their cattle to find new grazing on the **savannah** in Kenya.

Today, the Maasai are facing problems. **Droughts** in East Africa are causing water shortages. The drought in December 2006 was the worst in living memory. Many Maasai lost their animals. There was not enough water to keep them alive.

Following the drought in 2006, much of East Africa was flooded. People had to be air-lifted to safety.

▲ A Maasai man walks past the skeleton of a dead animal, which died as a result of the drought.

FARMING LAND

Traditionally, the Maasai did not dig up their land. They believed that land used to grow **crops** was wasted. They preferred cattle to **graze** (feed) on the land. Today, many Maasai have to grow crops such as **maize** (corn) to survive.

Maasai warriors

The Maasai have long been known as fierce and fearless warriors. Maasai boys go through many ceremonies as they grow up to become warriors. Maasai boys and men are divided up into groups of a similar age. These groups are called age-sets. Maasai men and boys move from one stage to the next with their own age-set.

MANYATTA

Young warriors are known as **morani**. They spend years living in a warrior camp, called *manyatta*. This teaches them to live away from home. They learn how to look after their cattle. They also learn how to protect their community.

▲ Maasai boys take part in a warrior ceremony in Kenya.

▲ Maasai warriors cover their shaved heads with red earth as part of a ceremony.

A young warrior is called a *moran*. He looks after the cattle. Every ten or so years, all the warriors in an age-set become senior warriors. They are told: "Now that you are an **elder**, drop your weapons. Use your head and wisdom instead." The senior warriors are allowed to marry and start families.

At home

Maasai homes are built by the women. Between 10 and 20 small huts are built together. The huts form a **settlement** called an *enkang*. A settlement is a place where people live.

The men make fences out of sharp thorn bush branches. The fences surround the *enkang*. The fences keep the precious cattle in. They also keep out hungry **predators**, such as lions. Predators are animals that kill and eat other animals.

▶ Here are Maasai huts in an *enkang* in Tanzania.

WHO LIVES WHERE?

Maasai women share their huts and beds with their children and grandchildren. Men live separately, in different huts.

▲ Maasai women use grass to tie together the wooden frame of a hut in Kenya.

A Maasai woman has to learn how to build her hut. She uses branches tied with strips of bark and grass. These make a strong frame. She often stuffs dried grass and leaves into the frame for **insulation**. Insulation keeps the hut at a regular temperature. She then mixes cow dung with urine and mud. This covers the frame. The cow dung mixture bakes hard in the hot sun.

Family life

Maasai women build and repair their huts. They also collect firewood and water, wash clothes, and milk the cattle. They cook meals for their families and care for the children.

In recent times, finding and fetching water has often been difficult. This is because the lack of rainfall has led to **droughts**. Women sometimes walk many kilometres a day to bring back water. Maasai children help their parents by looking after the sheep and goats.

▼ Maasai girls carry water in plastic containers back to their homes.

LAND

Since the 1960s, a lot of the land used by the Maasai to **graze** their cattle has been taken away. Some has been turned into farmland. Large areas have become **national parks**. The Maasai are no longer allowed to graze their animals in these places.

▲ A Maasai boy looks after a herd of goats in Kenya.

Maasai men protect the *enkang* (village) and their cattle. They must also find good grazing land for their cattle. They often walk for many days to look for fresh grazing areas.

Older men are in charge of the Maasai community. They organize activities and decide who should do them.

Food and eating

Traditionally, the Maasai have relied on their animals for food. They drink milk from their cattle and other animals. They keep the milk in decorated **gourds**. These are containers made from large fruits. The gourds are hollowed out and dried. The Maasai eat meat from their sheep and goats. They do not usually eat meat from their cattle. They also eat honey and porridge, and drink spicy *chai* (tea).

▲ A Maasai woman milks her cows. Milk is an important part of the Maasai diet.

HUNTING

The Maasai do not hunt wild animals for their meat. But they sometimes kill wild animals that attack their cattle. In the past, young warriors were taught how to hunt lions. This has now stopped.

◂ After a long drought in 2006, Maasai women wait to collect sacks of food from an aid agency.

Today, the numbers of cattle have fallen. The Maasai have been forced to look elsewhere for food. Many Maasai now buy food from markets or grow **crops**. They eat **maize** (corn), rice, and vegetables such as potatoes and cabbage. During times of **drought**, **aid agencies** help the Maasai. Aid agencies are organizations that give food and supplies to people in need.

Clothes and beadwork

Maasai clothing is mostly red. Young warriors (*morani*) wear short red skirts. They grow and plait their hair. They smear their hair with **ochre**. Ochre is red mud mixed with animal fat. When the *morani* become senior warriors, their hair is shaved off.

Older men wear red robes and a kind of **shawl** (blanket) around their shoulders. This is called a *shukka*. Married women wear blue clothes.

▶ The hair of this young Maasai warrior is plaited and covered with ochre.

Maasai women make beautiful, coloured beadwork. In the past, they made beads from shells, seeds, and clay. Today, they buy coloured glass or plastic beads. They make elaborate necklaces, bracelets, and earrings. Beadwork is worn by both women and men. It is also sold to tourists.

▲ Maasai girls and women wear elaborate necklaces and earrings.

WEARING BEADWORK

The Maasai wear necklaces and earrings for their beauty. They also wear them for special occasions, such as weddings or ceremonies. A girl wears a knee-length necklace for her wedding. It can be so heavy that she can hardly walk!

Make a Maasai bracelet

The colours and designs of Maasai beadwork have many meanings. Young women, married women, warriors, and **elders** have their own special patterns. Try making this simple Maasai bracelet.

You will need:

- stretchy bead elastic thread
- pliers (ask an adult to use these)
- scissors
- crimp beads (special craft metal beads)
- coloured beads

crimp beads

1. Measure around your wrist and then add 15 cm (6 inches) to this measurement. Cut three of these lengths of stretchy bead elastic thread.

2. Thread a crimp bead over the three threads. Ask an adult to squeeze the crimp bead closed with pliers, about 6 cm (2 inches) from the end. The crimp bead will hold the threads and beads in place. Now you can start adding the beads.

3. Add a few bigger beads as decoration, and some more crimp beads to hold the beads in place. Lastly, add a final crimp bead about 6 cm (2 inches) from the other end, to secure the bracelet.

COLOURS

The Maasai give colours special meanings. Red is the most important colour because it is the colour of a cow's blood. Blue is the colour of the sky. Precious rain falls from the sky. Green is the colour of the grass on which cattle **graze** (feed). White is the colour of milk. Milk is a favourite food of the Maasai.

Now you are ready to tie on the bracelet to your wrist.

School and language

In the past, most Maasai children did not go to school. This is partly because they often moved around. Also, many Maasai parents did not want their children to go to school. They thought their children would forget the Maasai **customs** and ways of life. These traditions make up their **culture**.

▶ In schools today, Maasai children learn Swahili and English. They also speak the Maasai language, *Olmaa*.

Today this opinion is changing. Many Maasai now see education as a way to **preserve** (keep) their culture. For example, the Maasai speak their own language, called *Olmaa*. But other people in Kenya and Tanzania speak **Swahili** and English. The Maasai need to speak these languages too. It means they can talk to other people about issues, such as land.

Count to ten in the Maasai language, *Olmaa*

One, *Nabo*

Two, *Are*

Three, *Uni*

Four, *Onguan*

Five, *Imiet*

Six, *Ile*

Seven, *Napishana*

Eight, *Isiet*

Nine, *Naudo*

Ten, *Tomon*

four

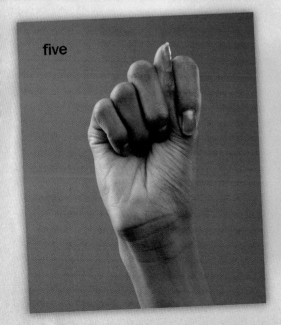
five

◀ ▶ As well as saying the numbers, Maasai also make finger signs to show the numbers. Try making these numbers.

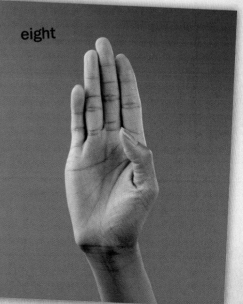
eight

Music and dance

Maasai music is based on the human voice. Songs are sung by groups of men and groups of women. Men sing about their cattle, hunting, and their bravery. Women sing lullabies or milking songs. They sing about their men and their children as well. Prayers are also sung as songs.

▾ A group of Maasai women stand side by side to sing a song.

In the past, the Maasai did not play any musical instruments. Today, people from different **cultures** and backgrounds have brought them new kinds of music. Some Maasai now sing Christian **hymns**. They can be sung along to drums or guitars. Other Maasai also sing songs in the **Swahili** language.

▸ Jumping is a test of strength, and it's fun too!

JUMPING COMPETITIONS

Singing is often accompanied by dance. The young warriors (*morani*) are well known for a special dance. They stand in a circle and sing. Each warrior in turn goes into the middle of the circle. He jumps up and down, on both legs. Some *morani* jump very high. These dances can go on for many hours.

Ceremonies

The Maasai have many ceremonies. They mark important moments in a person's life. A baby has a naming ceremony. It happens up to three years after birth. At the ceremony, the baby's and the mother's heads are shaved. A special bracelet is put on the child's right hand.

▶ This Maasai mother and child live in Tanzania.

Marriage is another important ceremony. A man shows interest in a girl by giving her a special chain. He gives gifts of honey and milk to her family. On the wedding day, the groom brings cattle and sheep to the bride's family. The bride wears a sheepskin dress. During the ceremony, her head is shaved. She stays at the home of her new husband's mother. After two days the couple are considered married.

▲ A young Maasai woman wears elaborate beadwork necklaces, headdress, and earrings during her marriage ceremony.

EUNOTO

A special ceremony marks young warriors (**morani**) turning into senior warriors. This is called *eunoto*. All *morani* grow their hair. During the ceremony, the mothers of the *morani* shave off this long hair. This shows that each warrior's youth is now in the past.

A Maasai story

There is a place in Kenya called Mashuru. It is beside the Eselenkei River. Standing among some tall acacia trees is a large stone. The stone looks almost like a person resting under the trees. The Maasai have a **legend** linked to this stone called "The maiden".

▼ The daughter of a Maasai elder looked after his animals.

The maiden

Many years ago, a Maasai **elder** lived with his daughter. She looked after his animals. One day, the young girl was out with the cattle. A group of young warriors (*morani*) started to talk to her. As they spoke, her father's cattle wandered off. The girl did not notice.

Later, the father went looking for his daughter and animals. After a long search he found the girl. She was still chatting with the *morani*. He was angry that she had lost his cattle. He snapped, *"Taa osiot!"* This means, "Become a stone!" The girl turned into solid rock. Later, the river running by her feet was named Eselenkei. This means "the maiden".

◀ The girl started talking to a group of young warriors and forgot about the animals. The animals wandered off.

Find out for yourself

Books to read

Facing the Lion: Growing Up Maasai on the African Savanna
Joseph Lemasolai Lekuton and Herman J. Viola,
(National Geographic Books, 2005)
The Warrior and the Moon: Spirit of the Maasai Nick Would,
(Frances Lincoln, 2001)

Websites

www.laleyio.com/maasai.html
Learn about the Maasai people of East Africa.

www.maasai-association.org/welcome.html
Website of the Maasai association

www.maasaieducation.org/index.htm
Maasai Education Discovery website

www.maasai-music.com/index.php
Find out about Maasai music.

www.survival-international.org/tribes.php?tribe_id=12
Survival International information about the Maasai

Disclaimer
All the Internet addresses (URLs) given in this book were valid at the time of going to press. However, due to the dynamic nature of the Internet, some addresses may have changed, or sites may have ceased to exist since publication. While the author and publishers regret any inconvenience this may cause readers, no responsibility for any such changes can be accepted by either the author or the publishers. It is recommended that adults supervise children on the Internet.

Glossary

aid agency charity or similar organization that provides food and other important goods to people in need

clan group of families who are related to each other

crop plant that is grown for food, such as a vegetable or fruit

culture customs and ways of life of a particular group of people

custom practice followed by a group of people

drought long period in which little or no rain falls

elder senior Maasai warrior

gourd container made from a large fruit that has been hollowed out and dried

grazing feeding by animals. Also used to mean land that has grass for animals to eat.

hymn song of praise

insulation layer of material that prevents heat from escaping

legend ancient, traditional story

maize corn

moran (more than one: *morani*) a young Maasai warrior

national park area of land that is protected by the government because of its natural beauty and wildlife

ochre red dye that comes from earth

predator animal that kills and eats other animals

preserve care for something in order to make sure that it is not changed or damaged

reserve area of land where animals are protected

savannah grassland

semi-arid climate that is hot or warm, with rainy seasons at certain times of year

semi-nomadic way of life in which people move from place to place at certain times of year. They search for grazing for their herds of animals.

settlement place where people have settled and built their homes

shawl blanket-like material worn round shoulders

Swahili language spoken by many people in East Africa

Index